General Information about Terrorism

Terrorism is the use of force or violence against persons or property in violation of the criminal laws of the United States for purposes of intimidation, coercion, or ransom. Terrorists often use threats to:

- Create fear among the public.

- Try to convince citizens that their government is powerless to prevent terrorism.

- Get immediate publicity for their causes.

Acts of terrorism include threats of terrorism; assassinations; kidnappings; hijackings; bomb scares and bombings; cyber attacks (computer-based); and the use of chemical, biological, nuclear and radiological weapons.

High-risk targets for acts of terrorism include military and civilian government facilities, international airports, large cities, and high-profile landmarks. Terrorists might also target large public gatherings, water and food supplies, utilities, and corporate centers. Further, terrorists are capable of spreading fear by sending explosives or chemical and biological agents through the mail.

Within the immediate area of a terrorist event, you would need to rely on police, fire, and other officials for instructions. However, you can prepare in much the same way you would prepare for other crisis events.

The following are general guidelines:

- Be aware of your surroundings.

- Move or leave if you feel uncomfortable or if something does not seem right.

- Take precautions when traveling. Be aware of conspicuous or unusual behavior. Do not accept packages from strangers. Do not leave luggage unattended. You should promptly report unusual behavior, suspicious or unattended packages, and strange devices to the police or security personnel.

- Learn where emergency exits are located in buildings you frequent. Plan how to get out in the event of an emergency.

- Be prepared to do without services you normally depend on—electricity, telephone, natural gas, gasoline pumps, cash registers, ATMs, and Internet transactions.

- Work with building owners to ensure the following items are located on each floor of the building:

    - Portable, battery-operated radio and extra batteries.

    - Several flashlights and extra batteries.

    - First aid kit and manual.

    - Hard hats and dust masks.

    - Fluorescent tape to rope off dangerous areas.

Explosions

Terrorists have frequently used explosive devices as one of their most common weapons. Terrorists do not have to look far to find out how to make explosive devices; the information is readily available in books and other information sources. The materials needed for an explosive device can be found in many places including variety, hardware, and auto supply stores. Explosive devices are highly portable using vehicles and humans as a means of transport. They are easily detonated from remote locations or by suicide bombers.

Conventional bombs have been used to damage and destroy financial, political, social, and religious institutions. Attacks have occurred in public places and on city streets with thousands of people around the world injured and killed.

Parcels that should make you suspicious:

- Are unexpected or from someone unfamiliar to you.
- Have no return address, or have one that can't be verified as legitimate.
- Are marked with restrictive endorsements such as "Personal," "Confidential," or "Do not X-ray."
- Have protruding wires or aluminum foil, strange odors, or stains.
- Show a city or state in the postmark that doesn't match the return address.
- Are of unusual weight given their size, or are lopsided or oddly shaped.
- Are marked with threatening language.
- Have inappropriate or unusual labeling.
- Have excessive postage or packaging material, such as masking tape and string.
- Have misspellings of common words.
- Are addressed to someone no longer with your organization or are otherwise outdated.
- Have incorrect titles or titles without a name.
- Are not addressed to a specific person.
- Have hand-written or poorly typed addressess.

Take Protective Measures

If you receive a telephoned bomb threat, you should do the following:

- Get as much information from the caller as possible.

- Keep the caller on the line and record everything that is said.

- Notify the police and the building management.

If there is an explosion, you should:

- Get under a sturdy table or desk if things are falling around you. When they stop falling, leave quickly, watching for obviously weakened floors and stairways. As you exit from the building, be especially watchful of falling debris.

- Leave the building as quickly as possible. Do not stop to retrieve personal possessions or make phone calls.

- Do not use elevators.

Once you are out:

- Do not stand in front of windows, glass doors, or other potentially hazardous areas.

- Move away from sidewalks or streets to be used by emergency officials or others still exiting the building.

During an Explosion

Safety guidelines for escaping fires in Section 2.11

If you are trapped in debris:

- If possible, use a flashlight to signal your location to rescuers.

- Avoid unnecessary movement so you don't kick up dust.

- Cover your nose and mouth with anything you have on hand. (Dense-weave cotton material can act as a good filter. Try to breathe through the material.)

- Tap on a pipe or wall so rescuers can hear where you are.

- If possible, use a whistle to signal rescuers.

- Shout only as a last resort. Shouting can cause a person to inhale dangerous amounts of dust.

Follow the instructions for recovering from a disaster in Part 5.

For More Information

If you require more information about any of these topics, the following resource may be helpful.

Publications

American Red Cross:

Terrorism, Preparing for the Unexpected. Document providing preparation guidelines for a terrorist attack or similar emergency. Available online at www.redcross.org/services/disaster/0,1082,0_589_,00.html

Biological Threats

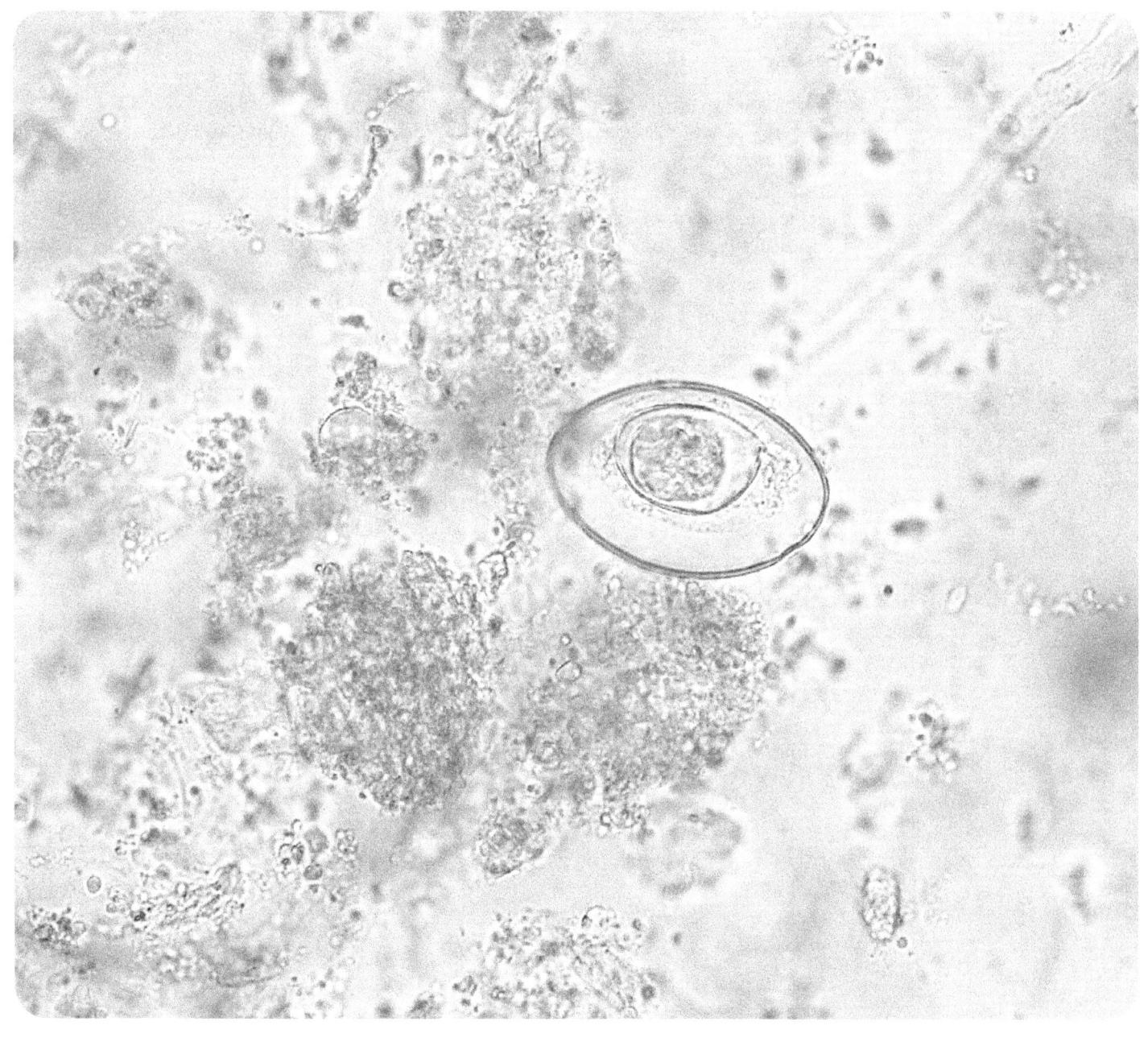

Biological agents are organisms or toxins that can kill or incapacitate people, livestock, and crops. The three basic groups of biological agents that would likely be used as weapons are bacteria, viruses, and toxins. Most biological agents are difficult to grow and maintain. Many break down quickly when exposed to sunlight and other environmental factors, while others, such as anthrax spores, are very long lived. Biological agents can be dispersed by spraying them into the air, by infecting animals that carry the disease to humans, and by contaminating food and water. Delivery methods include:

- **Aerosols**—biological agents are dispersed into the air, forming a fine mist that may drift for miles. Inhaling the agent may cause disease in people or animals.

- **Animals**—some diseases are spread by insects and animals, such as fleas, mice, flies, mosquitoes, and livestock.

- **Food and water contamination**—some pathogenic organisms and toxins may persist in food and water supplies. Most microbes can be killed, and toxins deactivated, by cooking food and boiling water. Most microbes are killed by boiling water for one minute, but some require longer. Follow official instructions.

- **Person-to-person**—spread of a few infectious agents is also possible. Humans have been the source of infection for smallpox, plague, and the Lassa viruses.

Specific information on biological agents is available at the Centers for Disease Control and Prevention's Web site, www.bt.cdc.gov.

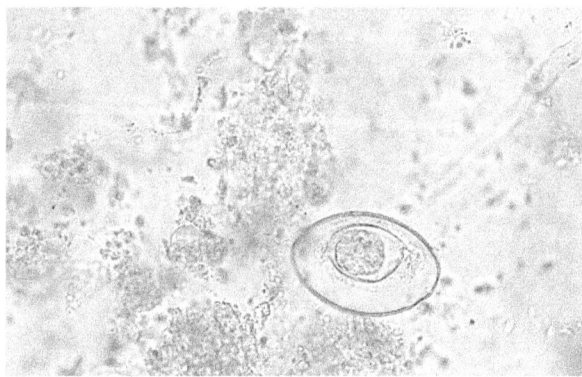

Take Protective Measures

Before a Biological Attack

The following are guidelines for what you should do to prepare for a biological threat:

- Check with your doctor to ensure all required or suggested immunizations are up to date. Children and older adults are particularly vulnerable to biological agents.

- Consider installing a High Efficiency Particulate Air (HEPA) filter in your furnace return duct. These filters remove particles in the 0.3 to 10 micron range and will filter out most biological agents that may enter your house. If you do not have a central heating or cooling system, a stand-alone portable HEPA filter can be used.

Review

Shelter
in Section 1.4

Filtration in Buildings

Building owners and managers should determine the type and level of filtration in their structures and the level of protection it provides against biological agents. The National Institute of Occupational Safety and Health (NIOSH) provides technical guidance on this topic in their publication *Guidance for Filtration and Air-Cleaning Systems to Protect Building Environments from Airborne Chemical, Biological, or Radiological Attacks.* To obtain a copy, call 1(800)35NIOSH or visit www.cdc.gov/NIOSH/publist.html and request or download NIOSH Publication 2003-136.

During a Biological Attack

In the event of a biological attack, public health officials may not immediately be able to provide information on what you should do. It will take time to determine what the illness is, how it should be treated, and who is in danger. Watch television, listen to radio, or check the Internet for official news and information including signs and symptoms of the disease, areas in danger, if medications or vaccinations are being distributed, and where you should seek medical attention if you become ill.

The first evidence of an attack may be when you notice symptoms of the disease caused by exposure to an agent. Be suspicious of any symptoms you notice, but do not assume that any illness is a result of the attack. Use common sense and practice good hygiene.

If you become aware of an unusual and suspicious substance nearby:

- Move away quickly.

- Wash with soap and water.

- Contact authorities.

- Listen to the media for official instructions.

- Seek medical attention if you become sick.

If you are exposed to a biological agent:

- Remove and bag your clothes and personal items. Follow official instructions for disposal of contaminated items.

- Wash yourself with soap and water and put on clean clothes.

- Seek medical assistance. You may be advised to stay away from others or even quarantined.

Using HEPA Filters

HEPA filters are useful in biological attacks. If you have a central heating and cooling system in your home with a HEPA filter, leave it on if it is running or turn the fan on if it is not running. Moving the air in the house through the filter will help remove the agents from the air. If you have a portable HEPA filter, take it with you to the internal room where you are seeking shelter and turn it on.

If you are in an apartment or office building that has a modern, central heating and cooling system, the system's filtration should provide a relatively safe level of protection from outside biological contaminants.

HEPA filters will not filter chemical agents.

After a Biological Attack

Review

Getting
Informed
in Section 1.1

In some situations, such as the case of the anthrax letters sent in 2001, people may be alerted to potential exposure. If this is the case, pay close attention to all official warnings and instructions on how to proceed. The delivery of medical services for a biological event may be handled differently to respond to increased demand. The basic public health procedures and medical protocols for handling exposure to biological agents are the same as for any infectious disease. It is important for you to pay attention to official instructions via radio, television, and emergency alert systems.

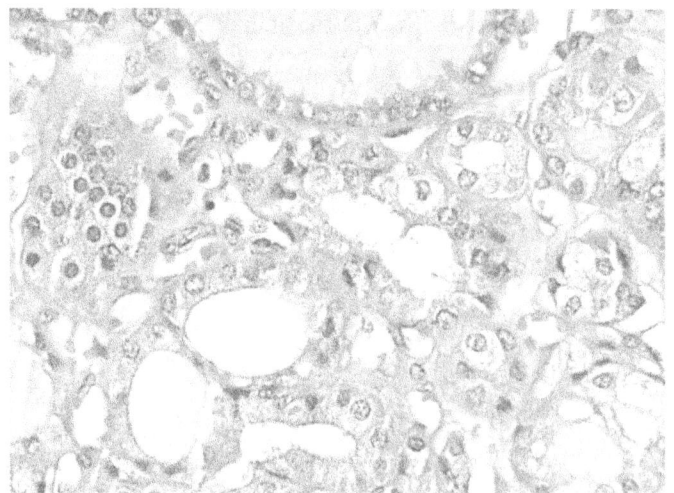

Chemical   Threats

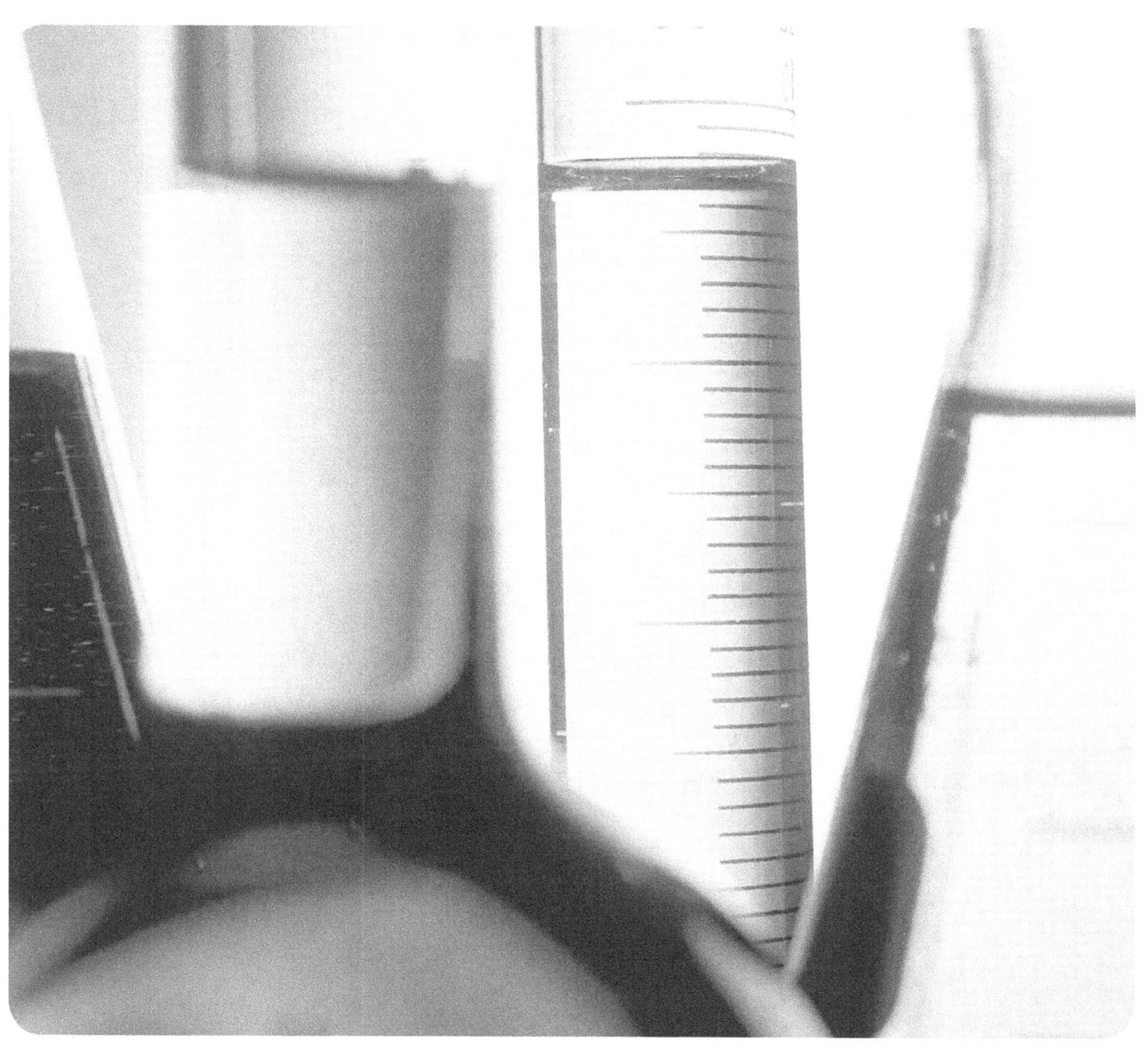

Chemical agents are poisonous vapors, aerosols, liquids, and solids that have toxic effects on people, animals, or plants. They can be released by bombs or sprayed from aircraft, boats, and vehicles. They can be used as a liquid to create a hazard to people and the environment. Some chemical agents may be odorless and tasteless. They can have an immediate effect (a few seconds to a few minutes) or a delayed effect (2 to 48 hours). While potentially lethal, chemical agents are difficult to deliver in lethal concentrations. Outdoors, the agents often dissipate rapidly. Chemical agents also are difficult to produce.

A chemical attack could come without warning. Signs of a chemical release include people having difficulty breathing; experiencing eye irritation; losing coordination; becoming nauseated; or having a burning sensation in the nose, throat, and lungs. Also, the presence of many dead insects or birds may indicate a chemical agent release.

Take Protective Measures

Before a Chemical Attack

The following are guidelines for what you should do to prepare for a chemical threat:

- Check your disaster supplies kit to make sure it includes:

  - A roll of duct tape and scissors.

  - Plastic for doors, windows, and vents for the room in which you will shelter in place. To save critical time during an emergency, pre-measure and cut the plastic sheeting for each opening.

- Choose an internal room to shelter, preferably one without windows and on the highest level.

During a Chemical Attack

The following are guidelines for what you should do in a chemical attack.

If you are instructed to remain in your home or office building, you should:

- Close doors and windows and turn off all ventilation, including furnaces, air conditioners, vents, and fans.

- Seek shelter in an internal room and take your disaster supplies kit.

- Seal the room with duct tape and plastic sheeting.

- Listen to your radio for instructions from authorities.

Review

Shelter safety for sealed rooms in Section 3.1

If you are caught in or near a contaminated area, you should:

- Move away immediately in a direction upwind of the source.

- Find shelter as quickly as possible.

Decontamination is needed within minutes of exposure to minimize health consequences. Do not leave the safety of a shelter to go outdoors to help others until authorities announce it is safe to do so.

A person affected by a chemical agent requires immediate medical attention from a professional. If medical help is not immediately available, decontaminate yourself and assist in decontaminating others.

Decontamination guidelines are as follows:

- Use extreme caution when helping others who have been exposed to chemical agents.

- Remove all clothing and other items in contact with the body. Contaminated clothing normally removed over the head should be cut off to avoid contact with the eyes, nose, and mouth. Put contaminated clothing and items into a plastic bag and seal it. Decontaminate hands using soap and water. Remove eyeglasses or contact lenses. Put glasses in a pan of household bleach to decontaminate them, and then rinse and dry.

- Flush eyes with water.

- Gently wash face and hair with soap and water before thoroughly rinsing with water.

- Decontaminate other body areas likely to have been contaminated. Blot (do not swab or scrape) with a cloth soaked in soapy water and rinse with clear water.

- Change into uncontaminated clothes. Clothing stored in drawers or closets is likely to be uncontaminated.

- Proceed to a medical facility for screening and professional treatment.

Nuclear Blast

A nuclear blast is an explosion with intense light and heat, a damaging pressure wave, and widespread radioactive material that can contaminate the air, water, and ground surfaces for miles around. A nuclear device can range from a weapon carried by an intercontinental missile launched by a hostile nation or terrorist organization, to a small portable nuclear devise transported by an individual. All nuclear devices cause deadly effects when exploded, including blinding light, intense heat (thermal radiation), initial nuclear radiation, blast, fires started by the heat pulse, and secondary fires caused by the destruction.

Hazards of Nuclear Devices

The extent, nature, and arrival time of these hazards are difficult to predict. The geographical dispersion of hazard effects will be defined by the following:

- Size of the device. A more powerful bomb will produce more distant effects.

- Height above the ground the device was detonated. This will determine the extent of blast effects.

- Nature of the surface beneath the explosion. Some materials are more likely to become radioactive and airborne than others. Flat areas are more susceptible to blast effects.

- Existing meteorological conditions. Wind speed and direction will affect arrival time of fallout; precipitation may wash fallout from the atmosphere.

Radioactive Fallout

Even if individuals are not close enough to the nuclear blast to be affected by the direct impacts, they may be affected by radioactive fallout. Any nuclear blast results in some fallout. Blasts that occur near the earth's surface create much greater amounts of fallout than blasts that occur at higher altitudes. This is because the tremendous heat produced from a nuclear blast causes an up-draft of air that forms the familiar mushroom cloud. When a blast occurs near the earth's surface, millions of vaporized dirt particles also are drawn into the cloud. As the heat diminishes, radioactive materials that have vaporized condense on the particles and fall back to Earth. The phenomenon is called radioactive fallout. This fallout material decays over a long period of time, and is the main source of residual nuclear radiation.

Fallout from a nuclear explosion may be carried by wind currents for hundreds of miles if the right conditions exist. Effects from even a small portable device exploded at ground level can be potentially deadly.

Nuclear radiation cannot be seen, smelled, or otherwise detected by normal senses. Radiation can only be detected by radiation monitoring devices. This makes radiological emergencies different from other types of emergencies, such as floods or hurricanes. Monitoring can project the fallout arrival times, which will be announced through official warning channels. However, any increase in surface build-up of gritty dust and dirt should be a warning for taking protective measures.

Electromagnetic Pulse

In addition to other effects, a nuclear weapon detonated in or above the earth's atmosphere can create an electromagnetic pulse (EMP), a high-density electrical field. An EMP acts like a stroke of lightning but is stronger, faster, and shorter. An EMP can seriously damage electronic devices connected to power sources or antennas. This includes communication systems, computers, electrical appliances, and automobile or aircraft ignition systems. The damage could range from a minor interruption to actual burnout of components. Most electronic equipment within 1,000 miles of a high-altitude nuclear detonation could be affected. Battery-powered radios with short antennas generally would not be affected. Although an EMP is unlikely to harm most people, it could harm those with pacemakers or other implanted electronic devices.

Protection from a Nuclear Blast

The danger of a massive strategic nuclear attack on the United States is predicted by experts to be less likely today. However, terrorism, by nature, is unpredictable.

If there were threat of an attack, people living near potential targets could be advised to evacuate or they could decide on their own to evacuate to an area not considered a likely target. Protection from radioactive fallout would require taking shelter in an underground area or in the middle of a large building.

In general, potential targets include:

- Strategic missile sites and military bases.

- Centers of government such as Washington, DC, and state capitals.

- Important transportation and communication centers.

- Manufacturing, industrial, technology, and financial centers.

- Petroleum refineries, electrical power plants, and chemical plants.

- Major ports and airfields.

The three factors for protecting oneself from radiation and fallout are distance, shielding, and time.

- **Distance** — the more distance between you and the fallout particles, the better. An underground area such as a home or office building basement offers more protection than the first floor of a building. A floor near the middle of a high-rise may be better, depending on what is nearby at that level on which significant fallout particles would collect. Flat roofs collect fallout particles so the top floor is not a good choice, nor is a floor adjacent to a neighboring flat roof.

- **Shielding** — the heavier and denser the materials—thick walls, concrete, bricks, books and earth—between you and the fallout particles, the better.

- **Time** — fallout radiation loses its intensity fairly rapidly. In time, you will be able to leave the fallout shelter. Radioactive fallout poses the greatest threat to people during the first two weeks, by which time it has declined to about 1 percent of its initial radiation level.

Remember that any protection, however temporary, is better than none at all, and the more shielding, distance, and time you can take advantage of, the better.

Take Protective Measures

Before a Nuclear Blast

Update your supplies; see Section 1.2

To prepare for a nuclear blast, you should do the following:

- Find out from officials if any public buildings in your community have been designated as fallout shelters. If none have been designated, make your own list of potential shelters near your home, workplace, and school. These places would include basements or the windowless center area of middle floors in high-rise buildings, as well as subways and tunnels.

- If you live in an apartment building or high-rise, talk to the manager about the safest place in the building for sheltering and about providing for building occupants until it is safe to go out.

- During periods of increased threat increase your disaster supplies to be adequate for up to two weeks.

Taking shelter during a nuclear blast is absolutely necessary. There are two kinds of shelters—blast and fallout. The following describes the two kinds of shelters:

- **Blast shelters** are specifically constructed to offer some protection against blast pressure, initial radiation, heat, and fire. But even a blast shelter cannot withstand a direct hit from a nuclear explosion.
- **Fallout shelters** do not need to be specially constructed for protecting against fallout. They can be any protected space, provided that the walls and roof are thick and dense enough to absorb the radiation given off by fallout particles.

Review

Shelter requirements in Section 1.4

During a Nuclear Blast

The following are guidelines for what to do in the event of a nuclear explosion.

If an attack warning is issued:

- Take cover as quickly as you can, below ground if possible, and stay there until instructed to do otherwise.

- Listen for official information and follow instructions.

If you are caught outside and unable to get inside immediately:

- Do not look at the flash or fireball—it can blind you.

- Take cover behind anything that might offer protection.

- Lie flat on the ground and cover your head. If the explosion is some distance away, it could take 30 seconds or more for the blast wave to hit.

- Take shelter as soon as you can, even if you are many miles from ground zero where the attack occurred—radioactive fallout can be carried by the winds for hundreds of miles. Remember the three protective factors: Distance, shielding, and time.

After a Nuclear Blast

Decay rates of the radioactive fallout are the same for any size nuclear device. However, the amount of fallout will vary based on the size of the device and its proximity to the ground. Therefore, it might be necessary for those in the areas with highest radiation levels to shelter for up to a month.

Review

Shelter requirements in Section 1.4

The heaviest fallout would be limited to the area at or downwind from the explosion, and 80 percent of the fallout would occur during the first 24 hours.

People in most of the areas that would be affected could be allowed to come out of shelter within a few days and, if necessary, evacuate to unaffected areas.

Remember the following:

- Keep listening to the radio and television for news about what to do, where to go, and places to avoid.

- Stay away from damaged areas. Stay away from areas marked "radiation hazard" or "HAZMAT." Remember that radiation cannot be seen, smelled, or otherwise detected by human senses.

Follow the instructions for returning home in Part 5.

Radiological Dispersion Device (RDD)

Terrorist use of an RDD—often called "dirty nuke" or "dirty bomb"—is considered far more likely than use of a nuclear explosive device. An RDD combines a conventional explosive device—such as a bomb—with radioactive material. It is designed to scatter dangerous and sub-lethal amounts of radioactive material over a general area. Such RDDs appeal to terrorists because they require limited technical knowledge to build and deploy compared to a nuclear device. Also, the radioactive materials in RDDs are widely used in medicine, agriculture, industry, and research, and are easier to obtain than weapons grade uranium or plutonium.

The primary purpose of terrorist use of an RDD is to cause psychological fear and economic disruption. Some devices could cause fatalities from exposure to radioactive materials. Depending on the speed at which the area of the RDD detonation was evacuated or how successful people were at sheltering-in-place, the number of deaths and injuries from an RDD might not be substantially greater than from a conventional bomb explosion.

The size of the affected area and the level of destruction caused by an RDD would depend on the sophistication and size of the conventional bomb, the type of radioactive material used, the quality and quantity of the radioactive material, and the local meteorological conditions—primarily wind and precipitation. The area affected could be placed off-limits to the public for several months during clean-up efforts.

Take Protective Measures

Before an RDD Event

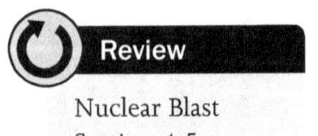

Nuclear Blast
Section 4.5

There is no way of knowing how much warning time there will be before an attack by terrorists using an RDD, so being prepared in advance and knowing what to do and when is important. Take the same protective measures you would for fallout resulting from a nuclear blast.

During an RDD Event

While the explosive blast will be immediately obvious, the presence of radiation will not be known until trained personnel with specialized equipment are on the scene. Whether you are indoors or outdoors, home or at work, be extra cautious. It would be safer to assume radiological contamination has occurred—particularly in an urban setting or near other likely terrorist targets—and take the proper precautions. As with any radiation, you want to avoid or limit exposure. This is particularly true of inhaling radioactive dust that results from the explosion. As you seek shelter from any location (indoors or outdoors) and there is visual dust or other contaminants in the air, breathe though the cloth of your shirt or coat to limit your exposure. If you manage to avoid breathing radioactive dust, your proximity to the radioactive particles may still result in some radiation exposure.

If the explosion or radiological release occurs inside, get out immediately and seek safe shelter. Otherwise, if you are:

Outdoors	Indoors
• Seek shelter indoors immediately in the nearest undamaged building. • If appropriate shelter is not available, move as rapidly as is safe upwind and away from the location of the explosive blast. Then, seek appropriate shelter as soon as possible. • Listen for official instructions and follow directions.	• If you have time, turn off ventilation and heating systems, close windows, vents, fireplace dampers, exhaust fans, and clothes dryer vents. Retrieve your disaster supplies kit and a battery-powered radio and take them to your shelter room. • Seek shelter immediately, preferably underground or in an interior room of a building, placing as much distance and dense shielding as possible between you and the outdoors where the radioactive material may be. • Seal windows and external doors that do not fit snugly with duct tape to reduce infiltration of radioactive particles. Plastic sheeting will not provide shielding from radioactivity nor from blast effects of a nearby explosion. • Listen for official instructions and follow directions.

After an RDD Event

After finding safe shelter, those who may have been exposed to radioactive material should decontaminate themselves. To do this, remove and bag your clothing (and isolate the bag away from you and others), and shower thoroughly with soap and water. Seek medical attention after officials indicate it is safe to leave shelter.

Contamination from an RDD event could affect a wide area, depending on the amount of conventional explosives used, the quantity and type of radioactive material released, and meteorological conditions. Thus, radiation dissipation rates vary, but radiation from an RDD will likely take longer to dissipate due to a potentially larger localized concentration of radioactive material.

Follow these additional guidelines after an RDD event:

• Continue listening to your radio or watch the television for instructions from local officials, whether you have evacuated or sheltered-in-place.

• Do not return to or visit an RDD incident location for any reason.

• Follow the instructions for recovering from a disaster in Part 5.

Terrorism Knowledge Check

Answer the following questions. Check your responses with the answer key below.

1   What would you do, if you were at work and…

    a. there was an explosion in the building?

    b. you received a package in the mail that you considered suspicious?

    c. you received a telephone call that was a bomb threat?

2   If caught outside during a nuclear blast, what should you do?

3   What are the three key factors for protection from nuclear blast and fallout?

4   If you take shelter in your own home, what kind of room would be safest during a chemical or biological attack?

5   In case of a chemical attack, what extra items should you have in your disaster supplies kit?

Answer Key

1. a. Shelter from falling debris under a desk and then follow evacuation procedures
    b. Clear the area and notify the police immediately
    c. Keep the caller on the line and record everything that was said

2.
- Don't look at the flash
- Take cover behind anything that offers protection
- Lay flat on the ground
- Cover your head

3. Distance, shielding, time

4. An interior room on the uppermost level, preferably without windows

5. Plastic sheeting, duct tape, and scissors.

Homeland Security Advisory System

The Homeland Security Advisory System was designed to provide a national framework and comprehensive means to disseminate information regarding the risk of terrorist acts to the following:

- Federal, state, and local authorities

- The private sector

- The American people

This system provides warnings in the form of a set of graduated "threat conditions" that increase as the risk of the threat increases. Risk includes both the probability of an attack occurring and its potential gravity. Threat conditions may be assigned for the entire nation, or they may be set for a particular geographic area or industrial sector. At each threat condition, government entities and the private sector, including businesses and schools, would implement a corresponding set of "protective measures" to further reduce vulnerability or increase response capability during a period of heightened alert.

There are five threat conditions, each identified by a description and corresponding color. Assigned threat conditions will be reviewed at regular intervals to determine whether adjustments are warranted.

Threat Conditions and Associated Protective Measures

There is always a risk of a terrorist threat. Each threat condition assigns a level of alert appropriate to the increasing risk of terrorist attacks. Beneath each threat condition are some suggested protective measures that the government, the private sector, and the public can take.

In each case, as threat conditions escalate, protective measures are added to those already taken in lower threat conditions. The measures are cumulative.

Citizen Guidance on the Homeland Security Advisory System

Low Risk

- Develop a family emergency plan. Share it with family and friends, and practice the plan. Visit www.Ready.gov for help creating a plan.
- Create an "Emergency Supply Kit" for your household.
- Be informed. Visit www.Ready.gov or obtain a copy of "Preparing Makes Sense, Get Ready Now" by calling 1-800-BE-READY.
- Know where to shelter and how to turn off utilities (power, gas, and water) to your home.
- Examine volunteer opportunities in your community, such as Citizen Corps, Volunteers in Police Service, Neighborhood Watch or others, and donate your time. Consider completing an American Red Cross first aid or CPR course , or Community Emergency Response Team (CERT) course .

Guarded Risk

- Complete recommended steps at level green.
- Review stored disaster supplies and replace items that are outdated.
- Be alert to suspicious activity and report it to proper authorities.

Elevated Risk

- Complete recommended steps at levels green and blue.
- Ensure disaster supplies are stocked and ready.
- Check telephone numbers in family emergency plan and update as necessary.
- Develop alternate routes to/from work or school and practice them.
- Continue to be alert for suspicious activity and report it to authorities.

High Risk

- Complete recommended steps at lower levels.
- Exercise caution when traveling, pay attention to travel advisories.
- Review your family emergency plan and make sure all family members know what to do.
- Be Patient. Expect some delays, baggage searches and restrictions at public buildings.
- Check on neighbors or others that might need assistance in an emergency.

Severe Risk

- Complete all recommended actions at lower levels.
- Listen to local emergency management officials.
- Stay tuned to TV or radio for current information/instructions.
- Be prepared to shelter or evacuate, as instructed.
- Expect traffic delays and restrictions.
- Provide volunteer services only as requested.
- Contact your school/business to determine status of work day.

*Developed with input from the American Red Cross.

Knowledge Check

1. By following the instructions in this guide, you should now have the following:

   - A family disaster plan that sets forth what you and your family need to do to prepare for and respond to all types of hazards.

   - A disaster supplies kit filled with items you would need to sustain you and your family for at least three days, maybe more.

   - Knowledge of your community warning systems and what you should do when these are activated.

   - An understanding of why evacuations are necessary and what you would need to do in the case of an evacuation.

   - Identification of where the safest shelters are for the various hazards.

   Compare the above actions with the personal action guidelines for each of the threat levels. Determine how well you are prepared for each of the five levels.

2. What is the current threat level? _____

   Hint: To determine the current threat level, check your cable news networks or visit www.dhs.gov. Keep your family informed when changes in the threat level occur, and go over the personal actions you need to take.

For More Information

If you require more information about any of these topics, the following resource may be helpful.

Publications

American Red Cross

American Red Cross: Homeland Security Advisory System Recommendations for Individuals, Families, Neighborhoods, Schools, and Businesses. Explanation of preparedness activities for each population. Available online at www.redcross.org/services/disaster/beprepared/hsas.html